TO WRESTLE WITH THE ANGEL

Sonnets from Petrarch's "Chapbook" of 1337

translations by

Lee Harlin Bahan

Finishing Line Press
Georgetown, Kentucky

TO WRESTLE WITH THE ANGEL

Sonnets from Petrarch's "Chapbook" of 1337

For Maura, Monica, and Marilyn

Copyright © 2018 by Lee Harlin Bahan
ISBN 978-1-63534-680-0 First Edition
All rights reserved under International and Pan-American Copyright Conventions. No part of this book may be reproduced in any manner whatsoever without written permission from the publisher, except in the case of brief quotations embodied in critical articles and reviews.

ACKNOWLEDGMENTS

"Response to a Poem Sent from Paris" and "Fardels" are featured in "Fathoming Petrarch," *Artful Dodge* 54/55.

"On Simone Martini's Portrait of Laura" first appeared in the Winter 2018 issue of *The Hudson Review*. The epigraph was added to *To Wrestle with the Angel*.

"Koheleth" and "Striving after Wind, with Honey," re-titled and revised for this chapbook, first appeared in *Natural Bridge*.

Scholarships to the West Chester University Poetry Conference let me study with Dick Davis in 2016 and take part in Tony Barnstone's 2017 Translation Seminar. Despite a crushing schedule, Tony made time to comment on translations in this chapbook: infelicities solely are due to my failure to heed his advice. I'm indebted to editors Paula Deitz, Ron Koury, Leah Maines, Kevin Maines, and Christen Kincaid for their kindness and flexibility during a personal crisis. Nor would I have accomplished much without help and encouragement from colleagues and friends old and new: Dan Bourne, Maryann Corbett, Rhina Espaillat, Becky Foust, Vince Gotera, Emily Grosholz, Sam Gwynn, Mike Juster, J. L. Kato, Ruth Killion, Susan McLean, Alex Pepple, Dick Pflum *(in pace requiescat)*, Tim Richardson, Toni Seger, Wendy Sloan, Alicia Stallings, and Shari Wagner, as well as husband Pat, with whom I hope to have many miles to go.

Publisher: Leah Maines
Editor: Christen Kincaid
Cover Art: "The Annunciation and Two Saints," Simone Martini (1284-1344) and Lippo Memmi (1291-1356), 1333, https://commons.wikimedia.org/wiki/File%3ASimone_Martini_and_Lippo_Memmi_-_The_Annunciation_and_Two_Saints_-_WGA15010.jpg
Author Photo: Pat Bahan
Cover Design: Elizabeth Maines McCleavy

Printed in the USA on acid-free paper.
Order online: www.finishinglinepress.com
also available on amazon.com

Author inquiries and mail orders:
Finishing Line Press
P. O. Box 1626
Georgetown, Kentucky 40324
U. S. A.

Table of Contents

Preface 1
On Simone Martini's Portrait of Laura 3
Second Thoughts on Martini's Portrait of Laura 4
Plutarch, Lucan, and Jashar 5
Psalms 37:35 6
Fardels 7
Koheleth 8
A Time to Pluck Up 9
A Time to Heal 10
No New Thing 11
Proposal, by Geri Gianfigliazzi 12
Response to Gianfigliazzi 13
Striving after Wind, with Honey 14
Response to a Poem Sent from Paris 15
Inspired by the Ninth Commandment,
    for the Day before Pentecost 16
First Voyage from Marseilles to Rome 17
Brown Surcoat, Green Silk Kirtle with Dagged Sleeves 18
Genesis 32:24 19
Proposal, by Pietro Dietisalvi 20
Response to Dietisalvi 21
Analogous to Caryatid 22
Ezekiel 19:3 and Revelations 3:16b 23
Responses to a Friend's Poem, Using Its Rhymes
    Ecclesiastes 3:1 24
    Twist and Turn 25
Sent with a Pillow, Book, and Cup to Agapito Colonna,
    Christmas 1337 26
Notes 27
Works Consulted 32

Petrarch's first collection of his *rime* consists, physically, of eleven pages written by him, chiefly or wholly within the period 1336-1337, and, in content, of the 25 poems transcribed thereon (23 composed by Petrarch, two by poet-friends of his)...

...This collection, since it lacks a principle of arrangement, cannot properly be considered as a first form of the *Canzoniere*...

Of the 22 sonnets of Petrarch extant in the first collection, seventeen passed ultimately into the *Canzoniere*, and five were ultimately rejected.... Four of the five rejected sonnets are *riposte*.

—Ernest Hatch Wilkins,
The Making of the Canzoniere *and Other Petrarchan Studies*

In placid hours well-pleased we dream
Of many a brave unbodied scheme.
But form to lend, pulsed life create,
What unlike things must meet and mate:
A flame to melt—a wind to freeze;
Sad patience—joyous energies;
Humility—yet pride and scorn;
Instinct and study; love and hate;
Audacity—reverence. These must mate,
And fuse with Jacob's mystic heart,
To wrestle with the angel—Art.

—Herman Melville,
"Art"

Preface

This project was inspired by "Petrarch's First Collection of His *Rime*," the fifth chapter of a book by Ernest Hatch Wilkins, cited on the chapbook epigraph page. Thanks to Wilkins, I became interested in the *Rime disperse* (*Rd*), Petrarch's lyric poems not in the work which he titled *Rerum vulgarium fragmenta* (*Rvf*). I was intrigued that the sonnets by "poet-friends" accompany Petrarch's pre-laureate responses—interactions that anticipate the poetry slam. Since I didn't find English verse translations of the five "rejected" *Rd* or of the two challenges to Petrarch's poetic prowess, I figured I'd found a promising place boldly to go.

My discoveries didn't disappoint, but raised a question, and the more I translated the more puzzled I became. I encountered in the *Rd* of Petrarch's first collection a young and hungry poet, but one otherwise familiar to me, whose classical allusions, themes, word play, and formal virtuosity seem of a piece with those of the artist as an older man. Why, then, did Wilkins dismiss this collection as an artwork? To fathom the respected scholar's opinion, I set about translating the seventeen sonnets that, differently ordered, were integrated into the final version of Petrarch's account of frustrated love for Laura.

Several months and a decent batch of translations later, I found a photo of a manuscript page containing the sonnet that opens Petrarch's first collection and became poem 77 of *Rvf*. The three sonnets on the page lacked titles or numbers, and an empty line separated one poem from the next. Each sonnet consisted of two columns of seven lines, resembling a newspaper, but was read across the page: first line of first column, first line of second column, second line of first column, and so on. I supposed the numbering of poems in *Rvf* was adopted to save scholars and critics the trouble of identifying each poem by its first line in Italian.

As I was about to concede that numbering Petrarch's poems probably skews perception of them less than do titles in the manner of Richard Tottel, I wondered if knowledge and appreciation of the structure of *Rvf* might hinder detection of structure in Petrarch's first collection. Might it be so evident that poems 45 and 46 of *Rvf* belong together, in this order, that their separation and reversed order in Petrarch's first collection would seem unplanned? For that matter, since Arabic numerals identify poems in *Rvf*, and Roman numerals identify *Rd*, which Wilkins labels "rejected," might not Roman numerals above *Rd* suggest their inferiority to poems in his masterpiece?

To shorten a long story, I believe that Petrarch's first collection constitutes what we today would call a chapbook. Since the physical form of Petrarch's sonnets long ago was "translated" from two columns of seven lines into one column of fourteen, I decided to "translate" Petrarch's first collection into a modern chapbook, chiefly by giving his poems titles and epigraphs that he might have given them if using such means to clarify or enhance a poem's content had been common in his century. Otherwise, though my take on Petrarch is unconventional, I aim to stay reasonably faithful to the original text while making concrete and figurative dramatic situations, as well as difficult allusions, plain to modern readers. When I've embroidered for the sake of the poem's music in English, I've tried to do so in a way not inconsistent with Petrarch's meaning in that instance, and with what I know of his work in general. Because seven of the sonnets in Petrarch's first collection aren't well known, and to keep me honest, each translation appears above its Italian text in its original physical form, without number or title.

In addition to identifying each of Petrarch's poems by *Rvf* or *Rd* number, the notes are meant to function as a trail of bread crumbs leading readers to understand and evaluate my construction of Petrarch's first collection. Interpreting Petrarch demands that I go outside his text; just because "it" isn't on Petrarch's page, doesn't mean "it" didn't appear before the mind's eyes of his medieval readers. Money says that you'll experience a similar phenomenon, when, coming upon a certain word in this chapbook, you'll think of an author, though that person's name appears nowhere on the page involved. Granted, the original poem in question doesn't indirectly direct the reader's attention in the specific way that I do in my translation, but Petrarch performs this sort of legerdemain elsewhere in this collection and often. Hopefully, the map of my intuitive process, to allude to a recent Google Doodle, isn't redolent of burnt toast.

Now I will pretend to disappear, and let a talented young poet introduce himself to you. I think you'll find that the work in this first collection is ambitious and has staying power. Francesco Petrarca has a long, bright future ahead of him.

Lee Harlin Bahan
14 February 2018

On Simone Martini's Portrait of Laura

> *These artists… have joined in a trial of skill in the Amazons which they have respectively made.*
> —Pliny the Elder, *Natural History, 34.19*

Were Polykleitos and his fellow sculptors
to try to see whose eye was best, they wouldn't
catch the least part of the beauty sent
to conquer my heart, not in a thousand years.

But my Simone was in heaven for sure
when he spied this gentle emigrant
and put her on a page to document
the sheer perfection of her features here.

The work is one of those you very well
could picture in the sky, not with us where
members of the body veil the soul.

It was a favor; nor could he do it after
he'd come down to take on heat and cold
and felt mortal at the sight of her.

Per mirar Policleto a prova fiso
mill' anni non vedrian la minor parte
Ma certo il mio Simon fu in Paradiso
ivi la vide, et la ritrasse in carte
L'opra fu ben di quelle che nel cielo
ove la membra fanno a l'alma velo;
che fu disceso a provar caldo et gielo
con gli altri ch' ebber fama di quell'arte,
della beltà che m'àve il cor conquiso.
onde questa gentil donna si parte;
per far fede qua giù del suo bel viso.
si ponno imaginar, non qui tra noi,
cortesia fé, né la potea far poi
et del mortal sentiron gli occhi suoi.

Second Thoughts on Martini's Portrait of Laura

> *caritas patiens est benigna est caritas non*
> *aemulatur non agit perperam non inflatur*
> —I Corinthians 13:4 (Vulgate)

When Simon got his big idea, which for
my sake put a pencil in his hand,
had it, in addition to a figure,
given the gentle work a voice and mind,

my chest would vent the many sighs that trigger
disgust for what others embrace: yet I find
humility expressed, giving her picture
the aura of promising me peace. She'd lend,

then, when I came to ply her with arguments,
an ear seemingly well-disposed toward all
I said, were she capable of response.

Pygmalion, what divine and immense
praise you received and owe, if your idol
gave you a thousand times what I want once!

Quando giunse a Simon l'alto concetto   ch' a mio nome gli pose in man lo stile,
s' avesse dato a l'opera gentile   colla figura voce ed intelletto,
di sospir molti mi sgombrava il petto   che ciò ch' altri à più caro a me fan vile.
Però che 'n vista ella si monstra umile,   promettendomi pace ne l'aspetto,
ma poi ch' i' vengo a ragionar con lei,   benignamente assai par che m'ascolte:
se risponder savesse a' detti miei!   Pigmaliòn, quanto lodar ti dei
de l'imagine tua, se mille volte   n'avesti quel ch' i' sol una vorrei!

Plutarch, Lucan, and Jashar

Julius Caesar, whose hands in Thessaly sped
to stain the earth with blood from fellow citizens,
wept when his son-in-law's head was brought to him,
its identifying features noted;
and the shepherd who put a hole in the forehead
of Goliath wept for his rebel kin,
and, eulogizing Saul, gave the mountains
of Gilboa good reason to be sad.

But you, whom pity never renders pale,
who are without exception on alert
against the bow that Love pulls uselessly,

see me racked with a thousand mortal hurts
though not a single tear so far has fallen
from your beautiful eyes, just contempt and fury.

Que' che 'n Tesaglia ebbe le man sì pronte
pianse morto il marito di sua figlia
e 'l pastor ch' a Golia ruppe la fronte
et sopra 'l buon Saul cangiò le ciglia,
Ma voi, che mai pietà non discolora
contra l'arco d'Amor che 'ndarno tira,
né lagrima però discese ancora

a farla del civil sangue vermiglia
raffigurato a le fatezze conte;
pianse la ribellante sua famiglia,
ond' assai può dolersi il fiero monte.
et ch' avete gli schermi sempre accorti
mi vedete straziare a mille morti
da' be' vostr'occhi, ma disdegno et ira.

Psalms 37:35

The native tree I mightily adored
for many years, so long as fair limbs didn't
scorn me, caused my feeble wit to bud
in its shade and grow out of what I suffered.

Once at the point where I no longer feared
such tricks, what had been sweet became wormwood,
and I aimed all my thoughts, that carp how badly
off they are, at one mark from then onward.

What will the sighing lover say when my
groundbreaking verse gives him another hope
and that, too, is dashed on her account?

"May no poet collect a wreath nor Jupiter
cast wide of it, and may the advent
of the sun in wrath suck all its green leaves dry!"

L'arbor gentil che forte amai molt'anni (mentre i bei rami non m'ebber a sdegno)
fiorir faceva il mio debile ingegno a la sua ombra et crescer negli affanni.
Poi che, securo me di tali inganni, fece di dolce sé spietato legno,
i' rivolsi i pensier tutti ad un segno, che parlan sempre de' lor tristi danni.
Che porà dir chi per amor sospira, s' altra speranza le mie rime nove
gli avesser data et per costei la perde? <<Né poeta ne colga mai, né Giove
la privilegi, et al sol venga in ira tal che si secchi ogni sua foglia verde!>>

Fardels

If I believed the love-filled thought that staggers
and fells me would empty when I died,
its contents long since would've accompanied
these irksome limbs into a grave I'd dug

by hand. But fearing tears and war would plague
me there, too, I stay halfway on this side,
sadly, of the passage I'm denied,
and half of me prostrate across it. I beg,

already well beyond late, for Love to send
the final arrow from the ruthless string
that other people's blood has rubbed and stained,

as well as her, who, hard of heart and hearing,
left me painted in her colors and
doesn't remember to call me to come along.

S' io credesse per morte essere scarco   del pensiero amoroso che m'atterra,
colle mie mani avrei già posto in terra   queste membra noiose et quello incarco;
ma perch' io temo che sarebbe un varco   di pianto in pianto et d'una in altra guerra,
di qua dal passo ancor che mi si serra   mezzo rimango, lasso, et mezzo il varco.
Tempo ben fora omai d'avere spinto   l'ultimo stral la dispietata corda
ne l'altrui sangue già bagnato et tinto,   et io ne prego Amore, et quella sorda
che mi lassò de' suoi color depinto   et di chiamarmi a sé non le ricorda.

Koheleth

The gold and pearls, the red and white flowers
that winter should have wilted and dried,
become for me sharp, toxic briars
that dig into my chest and rake my sides.

So my days will be tearful and fewer,
since great heartache rarely attains great age,
but I find more fault with lethal mirrors
that you've worn out, charmed by your image.

These mirrors cut short Love's attempts to win
you for me, left him speechless to discern
that you desire nobody but yourself;

these mirrors were made upstream of Hades' gulf,
permanently silvered with oblivion,
whereupon the cause of my death was born.

L'oro et le perle e i fior vermigli e i bianchi
son per me acerbi et velenosi stecchi
Però i dì miei fien lagrimosi et manchi,
ma più ne colpo i micidiali specchi
Questi poser silenzio al signor mio
veggendo in voi finir vostro desio;
d'abisso et tinti ne l'eterno oblio

che 'l verno devria far languidi et secchi
ch' io provo per lo petto et per li fianchi.
ché gran duol rade volte aven che 'nvecchi;
che 'n vagheggiar voi stessa avete stanchi.
che per me vi pregava, ond' ei si tacque
questi fuor fabbricati sopra l'acque
onde 'l principio de mia morte nacque.

A Time to Pluck Up

When the tree, which in human form repulsed
Apollo's advances, quits its peculiar space,
Vulcan breathes hard and sweats as he replaces
Jove's stock of relentless, jagged bolts,

who now thunders, now hails, and now pelts
us with rain, appearing not to honor Janus
less than Caesar; earth weeps and a sunless
sky shows he sees his dear friend somewhere else.

Then Mars and Saturn recollect their gall,
starry barbarians, and armed Orion waylays
hapless pilots, splitting helms and sails;

disoriented, Aeolus conveys
to Neptune and Juno, and to us, how it feels
when the fair face awaited by angels goes away.

Quando dal proprio sito si rimove
sospira et suda a l'opera Vulcano
il qual or tona or nevica et or piove
la terra piange e 'l sol ci sta lontano
Allor riprende ardir Saturno et Marte,
spezza a' tristi nocchier governi et sarte.
fa sentire et a noi come si parte

l'arbor ch' amò già Febo in corpo umano,
per rinfrescar l'aspre saette a Giove,
senza onorar più Cesare che Giano;
che la sua cara amica ved' altrove.
crudeli stelle, et Orione armato
Eolo a Nettuno et a Giunon turbato
il bel viso dagli angeli aspettato.

A Time to Heal

But when her sweet, slow, and self-effacing
smile doesn't hide its lovely novelty,
Sicily's smith produces no result,
flexing his ancient arms at Aetna's furnace;

because Jove has had taken from his grasp
arms tempered in Mongibello to the hilt,
Apollo's supervision can be felt
as youth creeps back into his mother's face.

A whisper from a western shore allays
the inexperienced pilot's fears, and tells
flowers in every meadow that it's day;

the sky empties of stars that don't bode well,
put to flight by her beauty and loving way,
owing to which untold tears have been spilled.

Ma poi che 'l dolce riso umile et piano
le braccia a la fucina indarno move
ch' a Giove tolte son l'arme di mano
et sua sorella par che si rinove
Del lito occidental si move un fiato
et desta i fior tra l'erba in ciascun prato;
disperse dal bel viso inamorato
più non asconde sue bellezze nove,
l'antiquissimo fabbro ciciliano;
temprate in Mongibello a tutte prove,
nel bel guardo d'Apollo a mano a mano.
che fa securo il navigar senza arte
stelle noiose fuggon d'ogni parte,
per cui lagrime molte son già sparte.

No New Thing

Latona's son, having looked from the vault
of heaven nine times already for a trace
of her who made him breathe hard to no purpose
and now takes the breath of someone else,

when, tired, with no one further to consult
regarding if she were far away or close,
appeared to us a man aggrieved to madness,
not finding that which he loved to a fault.

And thus sad he holes up, and misses welcoming
the face back that I'll praise one day
on quires of pages, pending my survival;

and she'd grown sorry for him anyway,
so tears sprang from her lovely eyes until
the air was, as in the beginning, wet and gray.

Il figliuol di Latona avea già nove
per quella ch' alcun tempo mosse in vano
poi che cercando stanco non seppe ove
mostrossi a noi qual uom per doglia insano
Et così tristo standosi in disparte,
sarà, s' io vivo, in più di mille carte,
sì che' begli occhi lagrimavan parte:

volte guardato dal balcon sovrano
i suoi sospiri et or gli altrui commove;
s'albergasse da presso o di lontano,
che molto amata cosa non ritrove.
tornar non vide il viso che laudato
et pietà lui medesmo avea cangiato
però l'aere ritenne il primo stato.

Proposal, by Geri Gianfigliazzi

Mr. Francesco, he who sighs because
he loves a lady still intent on war,
and the more he yells for mercy, the more
mean she is, hiding the two suns on which he's
most set,
        inspired by biology or reason,
tell him who sees himself treated as you are
whether he should leave her ranks, aware
there'll be Hades to pay if he does.

You and Love converse all the time,
and nothing about Him is unseen by you,
due to the superiority of your mind.

With Love forever, I think now I knew
Him better when, so let your brain tell mine
what to do: its true excuse will be yours said to.

Messer Francesco, chi d'amor sospira
et con' più merzé grida et più gli è fera,
qual che natura o scienza inspira,
trattar si vede, dite, et se da schiera
Voi ragionate con Amor sovente,
per l'alto ingegno de la vostra mente,
et men ch' al primo il conosce al presente,
per donna ch' esser pur vuolgli guerrera,
celandogli i duo soli che più desira
che deggia far colui che 'n tal maniera
partir si dee ben che non sia senza ira.
et nulla sua condizion so v'è chiusa
La mia che sempre mai collui è usa,
consigliate; et ciò fia sua vera scusa.

Response to Gianfigliazzi

Geri, when my sweet enemy, who is
so high and mighty, now and then gets sore
at me, one comfort saves me, except for
which my soul couldn't breathe: she rolls her eyes

all over the place to show how she despises
me and hopes to darken my life henceforward,
and then I show her my eyes truly lowered,
making her eat every scornful phrase.

If that weren't so, I'd be no more inclined
to go to see her than to face Medusa,
who turns people into marble. I'm

seeing your options limited to pursuing
my course because, when our Lord is behind
you, using His wings, to run has no value.

Geri, quando talor mecco s'adira
un conforto m'è dato ch' i' non pera,
ovunque ella sdegnando li occhi gira,
le mostro i miei pien d'umiltà sì vera
E ciò non fusse, andrei non altramente
che facea marmo diventar la gente.
ogni altra aita, e 'l fuggir val niente

la mia dolce nemica ch' è sì altera,
solo per cui vertù l'alma respira:
che di luce privar mia vita spera,
ch' a forza ogni suo sdegno indietro tira.
a veder lei che 'l volto di Medusa,
Così dunque fa' tu; ch' i' veggio esclusa
dinanzi a l'ali che 'l signor nostro usa.

Striving after Wind, with Honey

My enemy, the glass where you're used to seeing
your eyes reflect well on Love and Heaven,
doesn't charm you with its own attractions,
gentler and happier than a mortal being's.

It recommended, lady, that you fling
me from my sweet accommodation:
heartless exile! albeit my staying on
where you're alone might not be fitting.

But if driven nails put me in my place,
no mirror should make you hard and haughty,
pleased with yourself because I'm in pain.

Actually, if you recall Narcissus,
his course and yours approach one destination—
though no grass deserves a bloom that pretty.

Il mio adversario in cui veder solete
colle non sue bellezze v'innamora
Per consiglio di lui, Donna, m'avete
misero esilio! avegna ch' i' non fora
Ma s' io v'era con saldi chiovi fisso,
a voi stessa piacendo aspra et superba.
questo et quel corso ad un termino vanno—

gli occhi vostri ch' Amore e 'l Ciel onora
più che 'n guisa mortal soave et liete.
scacciato del mio dolce albergo fora:
d'abitar degno ove voi sola siete.
non dovea specchio farvi per mio danno
Certo, se vi rimembra di Narcisso,
ben che di sì bel fior sia indegna l'erba.

Response to a Poem Sent from Paris

Each day I make my face red and swarthy
often, thinking of tiresome, inflexible chains
in which the world has wrapped and so restrains
me from coming to keep you company.

Since it appears to my weak and untrustworthy
sight that some hope is what your hands contain,
I say, "There'll be a time, if I remain
alive, to return to the air of Tuscany."

Today I'm interned outside both demesnes,
so each vile creek's a giant obstacle,
and I'm a serf here, and liberty's a dream.

A crown of serviceberry leaves, not laurel,
weighs on my brow: now tell me you don't deem
your malady and mine almost identical.

Più volte il dì mi fo vermiglio e fosco
di che 'l mondo m'involve e mi ritene,
Ché pur, al mio veder fragile e losco,
e poi dicea: <<Se vita mi sostene,
D'ambedue que' confin son oggi in bando,
e qui son servo libertà sognando.
mi grava in giù la fronte: or v'adimando

pensando a le noiose aspre catene
ch'i' non possa venire ad esser vosco.
avea ne le man vostre alcuna spene;
tempo fia di tornarsi a l'aere tosco.>>
ch'ogni vil fiumicel m'è gran distorbo,
Nè di lauro corona, ma d'un sorbo
se 'l vostro al mio non è ben simil morbo.

**Inspired by the Ninth Commandment,
for the Day before Pentecost**

Though I've watched that you didn't make false claims
as much as possible, and honored you
lots, thankless tongue, you've not yet managed to
do me proud, but incited rage and shame:

since, when you'd help most to achieve my aims
by advocating mercy, you continue
growing icier, and words you do
form trail off . . . as if from a man who dreams.

And each night, sad tears, you accompany me
where I want privacy till dawn, then by
the time my peace comes, you've evaporated.

And you so quick to hurt and have me crying,
sighs, then drag yourselves out raggedly:
my face alone leaves nothing that I feel unsaid.

Perch' io t'abbia guardata di menzogna a mio podere et onorato assai,
ingrata lingua, già però non m'ài   renduto onor, ma fatto ira et vergogna;
ché quanto più 'l tuo aiuto mi bisogna   per dimandar mercede, allor ti stai
sempre più fredda, et se parole fai   son imperfette et quasi d'uom che sogna.
Lagrime triste, et voi tutte le notti   m'accompagnate ov' io vorrei star solo,
poi fuggite dinanzi a la mia pace!   Et voi, sì pronti a darmi angoscia et duolo,
sospiri, allor traete lenti et rotti!   Solo la vista mia del cor non tace.

First Voyage from Marseilles to Rome

> *And peals of thunder, with presaging sounds.*
> —Virgil, Aeneid

I knew well, Love, that following my gut
never would work against you: no
few snares and much I was told that wasn't so
had tried your lion-hearted grip a lot.

But recently, to get my awe to grow
(speaking as one involved, who witnessed what
occurred off Tuscany, where salt water cut
between shoreline and archipelago),

I slipped out of your hands, and hit the road,
winds and sky and waves unsettling me,
a no-one making my way somewhere sacred:

when—out of where remains a mystery—
there came your ministers, giving me to see it's bad
to tangle with and bad to hide from destiny.

Ben sapeva io che natural consiglio,
tanti lacciuol, tante impromesse false,
Ma novamente, ond' io mi meraviglio
et che 'l notai là sopra a l'acque salse
i' fuggia le tue mani et per camino,
m'andava sconosciuto et pellegrino;
per darmi a diveder ch' al suo destino

Amor, contra di te giamai non valse,
tanto provato avea 'l tuo fiero artiglio.
(dirol come persona a cui ne calse
tra la riva toscana et l'Elba et Giglio),
agitandom' i venti e 'l ciel et l'onde,
quando ecco i tuoi ministri, i' non so donde,
mal chi contrasta et mal chi si nasconde.

Brown Surcoat, Green Silk Kirtle with Dagged Sleeves

Apollo, if your exquisite desire
kindled by Thessalian foam still lives,
and if you haven't sent with the spinning years
her beloved blond hair to oblivion,

at the prospect of shiftless ice and severe
bad weather that, while you hide, won't break,
look out for leaves we honor and revere
today, where you first, and then I, got stuck,

and by virtue of the romantic hope
that sustains you in a life gone sour,
disencumber the air of every cloud,

so we then both will see a marvel: our
lady seated on the grass, arms up,
encircling her face, fingers linked for shade.

Apollo, s'ancor vive il bel desio
et se non ài l'amate chiome bionde,
dal pigro gelo et dal tempo aspro et rio
difendi or l'onorata et sacra fronde
et per vertù de l'amorosa speme
di queste impression l'aere disgombra;
seder la donna nostra sopra l'erba

che t'infiammava a le tesaliche onde,
volgendo gli anni, già poste in oblio,
che dura quanto 'l tuo viso s'asconde
ove tu prima et poi fu' invescato io,
che ti sostenne ne la vita acerba,
sì vedrem poi per meraviglia inseme
et far de le sue braccia a se stessa ombra.

Genesis 32:24

Alone, out late, at every ponderous step,
I gauge the most deserted battlegrounds,
and keep a sharp eye, meaning to escape
wherever human tracks depress the sand.

I otherwise have found no shield in face
of everyone's apparent recognition,
because a posture of snuffed happiness
spells out my inward conflagration.

So, I believe that shores, streams, woods, and crags
now understand that my life will be somewhat
hard, a thing hidden except from them;

but I know not to look for ways so rugged
and wild that Love doesn't always come,
having a word with me, and I with him.

Solo et pensoso i più deserti campi
et gli occhi porto per fuggire intenti
Altro schermo non trovo che mi scampi
perché negli atti d'allegrezza spenti
Sì ch'io mi credo omai che monti et piagge
sia la mia vita, ch'è celata altrui;
cercar non so ch' Amor non venga sempre

vo mesurando a passi tardi et lenti,
ove vestigio uman la rena stampi.
dal manifesto accorger de le genti,
di fuor si legge com'io dentro avampi.
et fiumi et selve sappian di che tempre
ma pur sì aspre vie né sì selvagge
ragionando con meco, et io con lui.

Proposal, by Pietro Dietisalvi

The fine eye of Apollo, in whose gaze
Juno senses a light both clear and shady,
wanting to demonstrate his potency
against a lady's disrespect for arrows,

attained noon's brilliance with incandescent rays
like warp on a vertical loom; nonetheless, he
didn't tarry, spying her gloriously
bright face, but fled the way a coward does.

Not seen in another without flaw before,
the beauty and fidelity that enliven
her planted a high and new love in his heart.

I don't know which of these joined and interwoven
two honors her or learned Phoebus more,
though: do perfect the places, then, where I fall short.

El bell'occhio d'Apollo, dal cui guardo
volendo sua virtù mostrar possente,
nell'ora che più luce il suo riguardo
ma quando vide il viso splendiente,
Bellezza et onestà che la colora,
furon cagion dell'alto et nuovo affetto.
più dotto Febo et qual più lei onora,

sereno et vago lume Iunon sente,
contr' a colei che non apprezza dardo
coi raggi accesi giunse orditamente;
senza aspettar fuggì come codardo.
perfettamente in altra mai non viste,
Ma qual di queste due unite et miste
non so: dunque adempite il mio difetto.

Response to Dietisalvi

If Phoebus didn't tell his first love lies,
nor new pleasure cause him to feel sorry,
the lovely laurel never will leave his memory,
casting shade that melts and turns me to ashes.

Only she dictates whether he rushes
or lags, is happy, sad, brave, or a sissy,
making him quake at her name apparently,
who shot until the serpent ceased to rise.

Nobody else distracted him when your
eyes opened to his fair face, which, even
when he changed appearance, were unhurt.

But our ladies may look, if yours has driven
the glow from his cheek, a bit alike: and I'm sure
you'll doubt that I'd say anything of the sort.

Se Febo al primo amor non è bugiardo
giamai non gli esce il bel lauro di mente
Questi solo il può far veloce e tardo,
ch' al suon del nome suo par che pavente
Altri per certo no 'l turbava allora
et non gli offese il variato aspetto.
sembianza è forse alcuna de le viste:

o per novo piacer non si ripente,
a la cui ombra io mi distruggo et ardo.
et lieto et tristo, et timido et valente,
et fu contra Fitòn già sì gagliardo.
quando nel suo bel viso gli occhi apriste
Ma se pur chi voi dite il discolora,
et so ben che 'l mio dir parrà sospetto.

Analogous to Caryatid

When on occasion, with reason to rage,
I surrender my usual humility,
which is to say, I lift eyes armed only
with faint scorn, since that's all I can manage,

instantly, one who is stronger looks down from her vantage,
and, shifting her gaze to meet mine, petrifies me,
set, as were Hercules' back and arms, to be
telamon to the heavenly entourage.

But then my virtue, dispersed to my outlying
parts, assembles in my heart to speed
its rehabilitation, pressed to sigh

and moan; my face assumes its former shade;
whereupon she holds back, ashamed to try
overcoming someone as good as dead.

Quando talor, da giusta ira commosso,
dico solo la vista, e lei stessa armo
ratto mi giugne una più forte a dosso
simile a que' per cui le spalle e l'armo
Allor però che da le parti estreme
per consolarlo, che sospira e geme,
ond'ella per vergogna si riteme

de l'usata umiltà pur mi disarmo,
di poco sdegno, ché d'assai non posso,
per far di me, volgendo gli occhi, un marmo
Ercole pose a la gran soma e 'l dosso.
la mia sparsa virtù s'assembla al core
ritorna al volto il suo primo colore;
di provar poi sua forza in un che more.

Ezekiel 19:13 and Revelations 3:16b

If you were able, by signaling malaise,
by dropping your gaze or bowing your head,
or bolting more quickly than Daphne did,
grimacing at fair, deserving pleas,

or via any other strategies,
ever to leave the spot where, deep inside
me, Love keeps grafting laurel branches, I'd
say your superciliousness had cause;

unsuited to a dry environment,
naturally a hothouse plant is pleased
to be uprooted and set down elsewhere.

However, since your destiny prevents
your being in other parts, do try at least
to stand forever someplace you can't bear.

Se voi poteste per turbate segni—
o per esser più d'altra al fugir presta,
uscir giamai, o ver per altri ingegni,
Amor più rami, i' direi ben che questa
ché gentil pianta in arido terreno
naturalmente quindi si diparte.
l'essere altrove, provedete almeno

per chinar gli occhi o per piegar la testa,
torcendo 'l viso a' preghi onesti et degni—
del petto ove dal primo lauro innesta
fosse giusta cagione a' vostri sdegni;
par che si disconvenga, et però lieta
Ma poi vostro destino a voi pur vieta
di non star sempre in odiosa parte.

Responses to a Friend's Poem, Using Its Rhymes

Ecclesiastes 3:1

Sometimes a knight knocks every foe to the ground
when fortune leads him to immense acclaim,
then against one, he buys life only with pain:
thus, seasons place feats in reach and out of bounds.

So possibly the one who this day lands
a death blow as yet may bear the other's pain,
if I can scrape up a little might and main,
or Love pulls his first arrow from my wound.

This hope feeds and saves my life from heat
to cold, from dawn till bells lure darkness back,
standing by as I wake, sleep, read, and write.

This hope soothes my injuries such that I take
no notice of them: I'm that keen to smite
him who breached me with one of her fair looks.

Tal cavalier tutta una schiera atterra
che da un sol poi si difende a pena:
Però forse costui ch'oggi diserra
s' i' posso un poco mai raccoglier lena
Di questa spene mi nutrico e vivo
con essa vegghio e dormo e leggo e scrivo.
ch'io non le sento, con tal voglia arrivo

quando fortuna a tanto onore il mena,
così 'l tempo apre le prodezze e serra.
colpi morta', ne porterà ancor pena,
o se del primo strale Amor mi sferra.
al caldo al freddo, all'alba et a le squille,
Questa fa le mie piaghe sì tranquille
a ferir lui che co' begli occhi aprille.

Twist and Turn

The one who sends the world's creatures to ground
and back to the elements whence they came
struck the knight, matter that entertains
all lands the isolating sea surrounds.

But this is a basilisk that whips and rounds
with ferocious eyes, bestowing death and pain
on men such that neither lance nor chain
can keep those who grapple with him sound.

The only remedy for his noxious look
is to arm yourself with mirrors so the light
returns like a spring-fed stream to a cleft rock.

He'll stop hissing and spitting at the sight
of himself maddened: if you want to make
this villa and others safe, do what I write.

Quella che gli animai del mondo atterra
percosse il cavalier, del qual è piena
Ma questo è un basilisco che diserra
tal che già mai né lancia né catena
Un sol remedio à il suo sguardo nocivo,
e torne quasi a la fontana il rivo:
quella sua rabbia: al modo ch'io ne scrivo

e nel primo principio gli rimena,
ogni contrada che 'l mar cinge e serra.
gli occhi feroci a porger morte e pena,
porian far salvo chi con lui s'afferra.
di specchi armarsi a ciò ch'egli sfaville
mirando sé conven che si destille
fia assicurata questa e l'altre ville.

Sent with a Pillow, Book, and Cup to Agapito Colonna, Christmas 1337

Rest your already tear-worn cheek on this,
my dear lord, and ever after be less free
to give yourself to one whose cruelty
renders a devotee's face colorless.

With another close the sinister pass
traveled by Love's messengers, and be
the same from August until January,
as time on a marathon is quick to pass.

And sip from the third the tincture of a plant
that purges every heart-afflicting thought,
sweet in the end, initially repellent.

Lock *me* up with your treasures so I won't
be terrified of Charon and his boat—
providing my suit's conceit is no impediment.

La guancia che fu già piangendo stanca riposate su l'un, Signor mio caro,
et siate ormai di voi stesso più avaro a quel crudel che' suoi seguaci imbianca;
coll'altro richiudete da man manca la strada a' messi suoi ch' indi passaro,
mostrandovi un d'agosto et di gennaro, perch' a la lunga via tempo ne manca;
et col terzo bevete un suco d'erba che purghe ogni pensier che 'l cor afflige,
dolce a la fine et nel principio acerba. Me riponete ove 'l piacer si serba
tal ch' i' non tema del nocchier di Stige— se la preghiera mia non è superba.

Notes

For unspecified Bible references, see American Standard Version (ASV).

Page 3: This poem became *Rvf* 77. See 1 Chronicles 29:15a and Joshua 10:12-13. The first scripture, true of Israelites who invaded and established Judaism in Canaan, is believed to be figuratively true of Christians. Second scripture is the first of two times that the Bible cites "the book of Jashar," and directly is revisited in *Rvf* 341.

Thomas Roche argues that the structure of *Rvf* is based on the Christian calendar. Roche suggests that *Rvf* 271 corresponds to January 1 of a leap year in which Good Friday falls on April 6. *Rvf* 77, then, corresponds to June 21, summer solstice. See notes for pages 9-11, page 16, and page 26.

Page 4: This poem became *Rvf* 78. The authorized version of the Bible in Petrarch's day was the Vulgate, Jerome's translation (excepting Ecclesiastes and a few other texts) of Hebrew and Greek sources into Latin. The epigraph and information are from Vulgate.org.

Page 5: This poem became *Rvf* 44. Modernity dawns when Petrarch compares the speaker's situation to "Great Man" versions of secular and Biblical history. See last paragraph of "Pompey, LXXX" of *Plutarch's Lives*, and see lines 1066-1080 of Walters' translation of Lucan's *Civil War*, Book Nine. Which account of Caesar's grief is true? Also see 1 Samuel 31:1-13 and 2 Samuel 1:1-27, especially verses 17 and 26 of the latter. Which account of Saul's death is true? Line 7 literally might be "scowled over the good Saul," which didn't match my Sunday School memories, sending me to the cited Bible chapters. Whether or not Jonathan's love for David was erotic, David's use of *brother* evokes *philos*, usually "brotherly love," but I think "familial love" is fair. In my view, the two poems that open Petrarch's first collection address *eros*, "sexual love," and *agape*, "divine love," while the third parallels *philos* and *eros*.

Page 6: This poem became *Rvf* 60. Compare Psalms 37:35 in ASV, Douay Version (DV), and King James Version (KJV). *Strong's Concordance* says the Hebrew *ezrach* means "Native (tree or person)." The DV is the English translation of the Vulgate. Canticles 5:15, DV, attributed to psalmist David's son Solomon, likens the male beloved to the cedars of Lebanon. It's curious, in the wake of Wyatt's and Surrey's translations of Petrarch, that the Protestant KJV renders *ezrach* as "bay," a synonym for *Laurus nobilis*, when referring to a wicked man. See note for pages 9-11.

Page 7: This poem became *Rvf* 36. How do you prove the translator alludes to *Hamlet*?

Page 8: This poem became *Rvf* 46. See Ecclesiastes 1:1-2. While at a college requiring a semester of Old Testament, I was told that *Koheleth*, rendered *Ecclesiastes* in the KJV, is Hebrew for "Preacher." I use the transliteration that Willis Barnstone does in his *Poets of the Bible*.

Pages 9-11: These poems became *Rvf* 41-43. See Ecclesiastes 3:2, Ecclesiastes, 3:3, and Ecclesiastes 1:9. The poems' rhyme patterns mirror seasonal change from winter storms to sunny spring weather to summer rain, roughly from winter solstice to summer solstice. Poems that may be associated with summer solstice and Christmas bracket Petrarch's first collection, suggesting the other half of the year.

    Having compared himself to psalmist (and adulterer) David, the speaker now identifies with Apollo, classical god of poetry, who fell in love with Daphne. Resisting, she cried for help, and her father, a river god, turned her into a laurel tree, thereafter sacred to Apollo. Petrarch endlessly puns on the similarity of masculine noun *lauro*, "laurel," to the beloved's name: the last vowel of *Laura* denotes a feminine noun, thus "female laurel." Note that the cursing in *Rvf* 60 gives way to pining, and Laura's contempt turns to pity: the relationship is deepening.

    Scholars differ regarding *sua sorella*, "his sister," in line 7 of *Rvf* 42. Robert Durling and Mark Musa say she is Latona, Apollo's mother and an earth goddess, but James Cook says she is Juno, the sister and wife of Jove. For several reasons, I went with Latona and "mistranslated" *sua sorella* accordingly.

Pages 12-13: Petrarch's response to Gianfigliazzi's proposal became *Rvf* 179. *Rvf* has 366 poems. Half of 366 is 183. According to Wilkins, the poem that became *Rvf* 179 is poem eleven of twenty-four sonnets in Petrarch's first collection, not counting spaces possibly left blank for more poems. (If you wondered, the twenty-fifth poem mentioned on the chapbook epigraph page was *Rvf* 23, a *canzone*, the transcription of which into the first collection only partially was completed.) Petrarch's response to Gianfigliazzi marks a movement (sometimes retrograde) toward "kinder, gentler" methods of gaining the beloved's affection. Emotional manipulation, though, leads to sublimation, artistic *hubris*, and (back) to the idolatry of *Rvf* 78. In a sense, putting women on pedestals violates the first of the Ten Commandments.

The proposals and responses in this collection illustrate how familial love, specifically what we today call "bromance," differs from a relationship involving sexual attraction. While it's fascinating to experience the medieval equivalent of a poetry slam, *Rvf* benefits from Petrarch's toning down of *philos*, which arguably lends coherence to his first collection, in favor of focusing on how *eros* complicates the human practice of *agape*.

Page 14: This poem became *Rvf* 45. My title combines elements of Ecclesiastes 1:14 and Proverbs 16:24; see note for page 16. I translated this sonnet about ten years ago, in the context of *Rvf*. There and then, *rival* was an acceptable, fresh take on *adversario*. In the context of Petrarch's first collection, though, the "enemy" meaning of cognate *adversary* better fits with *Rd* XVIII. Also see "Response to Gianfigliazzi," page 13. In *Rvf* 312, Laura "solely was [speaker's] light and looking glass" (L. H. B., *A Year OF Mourning*).

Page 15: Wilkins identifies this poem as *Rd* XVI. Wilkins uses Solerti's numbers for, and I use Solerti's Italian texts of, *Rd* in Petrarch's first collection.

Page 16: This poem became *Rvf* 49. See James 1:19-26, James 3:1-10, Acts 2:1-4, and Exodus 20:16. *The New Unger's Bible Dictionary* says Pentecost was a Jewish festival held seven weeks after Passover and associated with the giving of the Ten Commandments. That this poem became *Rvf* 49 hints that Petrarch's first collection anticipates the structure that Roche detects in *Rvf. L'aura*, "the air" or "the breeze," thus "gentle wind," was another of Petrarch's puns on *Laura*. See note for page 14.

Page 17: This poem became *Rvf* 69. See lines 245-266 of Dryden's translation of Virgil's *Aeneid*, Book Ten. Virgil was Petrarch's favorite author. *Ilva* is Latin for where Napoleon was able ere. The *Costa Concordia* sank off the island of Giglio in 2012. Imagine how young Petrarch felt in a storm on those dangerous waters where the Trojan fleet sailed to Aeneas' aid.

Page 18: This poem became *Rvf* 34.

Page 19: This poem became *Rvf* 35. In Chapter XVIII of *Making*, Wilkins says this poem "is derived from the elegy of Propertius… Book 1, No. 18." While Love in Petrarch's poems sometimes resembles Cupid, the Roman god of love, Wilkins' argument neither addresses Psalms 17:8 and 1 John 4:8, where the God of Abraham is described as winged and equated with love, nor looks at how *Rvf* 44, 179, and 69 relate to love's personification in *Rvf* 35.

Page 21: Wilkins identifies this poem as *Rd* XXVI.

Page 22: Wilkins identifies this poem as *Rd* VIII.

Page 23: This poem became *Rvf* 64. The concrete dramatic situation, in which Laura finds the speaker nauseating or she has morning sickness, is conflated with the Biblical image of Israel during the Babylonian Captivity, the image of the laurel growing in the desert of the speaker's heart, and the image of the Church as the Bride of Christ, held by Christians to be the successor to the Congregation of Israel and to be symbolized by the female beloved in Solomon's Canticles. During Petrarch's lifetime the Pope resided in Avignon, France, instead of Rome, and those who disapproved termed this state of affairs "The Babylonian Captivity."

Pages 24-25: Wilkins identifies these poems as *Rd* XVII and XVIII. The first poem of this pair implies that the speaker identifies with the knight. In the second poem the knight seems to have been defeated by Death, whose agent is a "dirty great snake" as Ron put it in the Harry Potter movie. The speaker, who identified with Apollo the slayer of Python in "Response to Dietisalvi," and who took issue with Laura's vanity, urges the reader to make the basilisk look in a mirror and be petrified by its own ugliness. "Response to Gianfigliazzi" and "Analogous to Caryatid" also have Freudian undercurrents. Perhaps the speaker is too ashamed (or proud) to confess in soul-sick first person. As Joseph Barber suggests, perhaps this pair of poems can't be understood without the proposal to which they respond.

Page 26: In footnotes to his translation of the poem that became *Rvf* 58, J. G. Nichols gives information used in my title, and says the poem is the "me" of the second tercet. Wilkins supplies the date. The recipient's name is a diminutive of *agape*, and well might be translated, "lesser divine love."

"August until January:" see notes for pages 9-11 and page 3. According to Roche's theory, *Rvf* 58 corresponds to June 2—as if Petrarch referred in his masterpiece's final form roughly to the end of the seasonal circle begun in his first collection.

Works Consulted

Barber, Joseph A., ed. and trans. *Francesco Petrarch: Rime disperse*. New York, NY: Garland Publishing, 1991.

Bostock, John, and H. T. Riley, trans. *The Natural History of Pliny*, vol. 6. London: Henry G. Bohn, 1857.

Clarke, Howard, ed. *Vergil's* Aeneid *and Fourth ("Messianic") Eclogue in the Dryden Translation*. University Park: Pennsylvania State University Press, 1989.

Cook, James Wyatt, trans. *Petrarch's Songbook*. Binghamton, NY: Medieval and Renaissance Texts and Studies, 1995.

Durling, Robert M., ed. and trans. *Petrarch's Lyric Poems*. Cambridge, MA: Harvard University Press, 1976.

Lucan. *Civil War*. Translated by Brian Walters. Indianapolis: Hackett Publishing Co., 2015.

Musa, Mark, trans. *Petrarch: The Canzoniere*. Bloomington, IN: Indiana University Press, 1996.

Nichols, J. G., trans. *Canzoniere*. New York, NY: Routledge, 2002.

Perrin, Bernadotte, trans. *Plutarch's Lives*, vol. 5. Cambridge: Harvard University Press, 1955.

Roche, Thomas P., Jr. "The Calendrical Structure of Petrarch's *Canzoniere*," Studies in Philology, 71 (1974), 152-172.

Solerti, Angelo, ed. *Rime disperse di Francesco Petrarca o a lui attribute, per la prima volta raccolte*. Florence: Sansoni, 1909.

Strong, James. *Strong's Exhaustive Concordance of the Bible*. Nashville: Abingdon Press, 1986.

Unger, Merrill F. *The New Unger's Bible Dictionary*. Chicago: Moody Press, 1988.

Wilkins, Ernest Hatch. *The Making of the "Canzoniere" and Other Petrarchan Studies*. Rome: Edizioni di storia e letteratura, 1951.

Francesco Petrarca, Petrarch to speakers of English, 1304-1374, was an Italian poet who grew up and spent a good bit of his life in and around Avignon, France. There, he claimed, he saw for the first time a beautiful, God-fearing, and married woman named Laura in church on Good Friday in 1327. By the end of 1337, he had assembled his first collection of lyric poems in Italian, and in 1341 was crowned poet laureate in Rome. Petrarch spent the next thirty years or so completing his masterpiece, variously known as *Canzoniere, Rime sparse,* and *Rerum vulgarium fragmenta,* chronicling its speaker's frustrated love for Laura while she lived and long after she died of bubonic plague in 1348.

Lee Harlin Bahan earned her MFA at Indiana University-Bloomington, where for six years she taught creative writing through the Division of Continuing Studies. She also has taught at DePauw University, Greencastle, IN, and been an Artist in Education for the Indiana Arts Commission. Lee has written two chapbooks, *Migration Solo* (Writers' Center of Indianapolis, 1989), and *Notes to Sing* (Finishing Line Press, 2016). *A Year of Mourning* (Able Muse Press, 2017), Lee's translation of a sonnet sequence in Petrarch's *Rerum vulgarium fragmenta,* was named a special honoree for the 2016 Able Muse Book Award. Local grant support and a residency at Mary Anderson Center for the Arts, Mt. St. Francis, IN, have furthered Lee's work as a translator. Her periodical credits include *The Hudson Review, The Kenyon Review, The North American Review,* and *Ploughshares.* When not writing, Lee enjoys quilting and canoeing. Pictures of her quilts and samples of her writing accompany an interview with Lee in the November 2017 Poetry Feature at *Through the Sycamores,* website of Indiana's 2016-17 Poet Laureate, Shari Wagner. Lee lives with her husband Pat on a farm outside Medora, IN.

www.ingramcontent.com/pod-product-compliance
Lightning Source LLC
LaVergne TN
LVHW040117080426
835507LV00041B/1295